Don't Frighten the Pansies

poems to inspire, entertain, and bring a smile

Don't Frighten the Pansies

poems to inspire, entertain, and bring a smile

Verna Cole Mitchell

Magnifico
Manuscripts

This book is a work of fiction. Names, characters, businesses, organizations, places, events, and incidents either are the product of the author's imagination or are used fictitiously. Any resemblance to actual persons, living or dead, events, or locales, is entirely coincidental.

Copyright © 2012 Verna Cole Mitchell

All rights reserved. Published in the United States by Magnifico Manuscripts, LLC Matthews, North Carolina
www.magnificomanuscripts.com

Cover and Book Layout and Design:
Stephanie Smith and Allie Tucker

Cover Photo: © 2010 Philip Barlow

Author Photo: © 2012 Leon Mitchell

ISBN 978-0-615-69184-8

Library of Congress Control Number 2012916480

PRINTED IN THE UNITED STATES OF AMERICA

Dedicated to my children and grandchildren,
more treasured than purest gold.

Acknowledgments

My thanks to:

My Lord and Savior for blessings too many to count

Lisa Mikitarian, Dee Yoder, and Beth Buff—my writing buddies, for their invaluable advice and their priceless friendship

Faithwriters for their weekly challenges to motivate me to write and for the encouragement of dear Faithwriter friends

Lorraine Fico-White, former neighbor, cherished friend, and still neighbor of my heart, for serving as editor and publisher, as well as advisor with just the right touch, and for gently prodding me to make this book into more than just a memory book for my children and grandchildren

My beautiful granddaughters, Stephanie and Allie, for using their talents to help me realize my dream of publishing

Mary Cole Ashby, my beloved sister, for being the best cheerleader a writer could have

My husband, Leon, for approving (or not) everything I wrote and for his love, a constant source of joy to me.

Contents

Introduction

A Taste to Savor   1

God's World

Don't Frighten the Pansies   5
Cloud Creations   7
Artist Almighty's Cloud Paintings   9
Creator's Concert Trio   11
Fall Feast   13
Foretaste   14
God's Music   15
His Survey   17
Lady Springtime   19
Nature at Play   21
Old Man Winter   23
Renaissance   25
Silent Symphony   27
Storm at Sea   29
Through My Window   30
Twilight of the Seasons   32
Viola Violet   34
Was Summer Made for Barefoot Boys?   36
In Motion by God's Hand   38

Inspiration

A Gloryland Eternity   41
A Job to Die for   42
A Mother's Blessing   43
A Picnic Breakfast   45
A Teacher's Prayer   46
Before the Beginning of Time   47

Brimful of Thanksgiving   48
I Taste the Grace   49
I Wonder   50
Keep Me in the Center of Your Will   51
Life's Blowouts   52
Morning Prayer   53
Praise Abounding   55
Rare Gems of Recollection   57
Road to Paradise   59
Simon's Soliloquy   61
Surety   64
That All May Know   66
This I Believe   68
Your God Has Not Forsaken You   70

Just for Fun

A Baptized Cat   73
A Feast of Manuscripts   75
A Tincture of Writer's Craft   77
Can You Feel My Pain?   79
A Touch of Gold   80
Come Go with Me to Join the Clown Parade   82
Fowl Play   83
Francina's Green Fever   84
Handout Hodgepodge   85
It's a Crime   87
Jealousy Is for the Birds   89
Miranda Ant   90
Monologue of the Merciless Editor   92
Muse Lost in the Library   94
Oh—It Hurts Just Thinking about It   96
Such a Fuss about Nothing   97
The Fool Has Said in His Heart   99
Won't You Have a Cookie?   101
Gabby Groceries   103
Bossy Bird   105

Reflections

A Family Christmas 109
Leon's Story 111
An Embarrassment of Blessings 113
And God Smiled 115
Artist of a Different Kind 117
Come with Me 118
Forever Sentry 120
Grandparents—Great, Great, and Beyond 121
Growing Old Charade 123
Guess Who 124
I Go for a Dip 126
Will You Still Hear Me Call Your Name? 128
In Apostle Paul's Footsteps 129
Into the Lion's Den 131
Kaleidoscope 133
Lessons from the Grandchildren 135
Now That Is a Great Adventure 137
Picture of a Queen 139
Shivering and Shuddering 141
Snapshots from a Teacher's Album 143
She Said 144
What Is It? 145

Introduction

A Taste to Savor

Come along with me
To a meal of poetry,
Where we will feast together,
You and I,
Upon reflections.
Lured by sirens of song
And aromas of rhyme,
We will make our way
To tables, top-heavy
With a smorgasbord of verse,
Minced and sliced,
Dried and diced,
Pruned and pureed,
Combined into tasty phrases
Of imagery—
Delectable tidbits
Of morsels of meaning,
Bitter and sweet together,
Stirred into sensory stews.
We'll ladle up lyrics,
Heaping appetizers of inspiration,
Rashers of romance,
And platters of personification.
We could almost make a meal
Of similes and metaphors,
Laced with alliteration,
And scattered with a sprinkling
Of vivacious verbs
And emotive modifiers—
All seasoned with wisdom and wit.
Never could there be
Another repast quite so savory,
Yet completely calorie free.

2

We will feed our artistic appetites
With nourishment for the soul.

God's World

Don't Frighten the Pansies

Be quiet, shhh, don't make a sound;
The earth is winter sleeping.
You'll frighten timid pansies that
Above the snow are peeping.

The squirrels, tiptoeing all around,
Are searching here and there.
They hid some nuts last autumn
But can't remember where.

Some bears and bats and skunks and snakes
Hide out in hibernation.
Away from cold, they rest in a
Restorative vacation.

Wee mice and moles beneath the ground
Are burrowed in their beds
With snow and icy covers as
Their ornamental spreads.

When God Creator will decree
Sweet springtime to arrive,
There'll be no need of shushing then;
The world will come alive.

The songbirds that in colder climes
Sing muted melodies
Will greet sun's dawning golden rays
With glorious symphonies.

Soft snowflakes, lightly touching down
On frozen bleak terrains,
Will be replaced by thunder's roar
And April's pounding rains.

The creek just now is frozen that
Meanders through the glen,
But with the sun's warmth thawing,
It will rush and roar again.

There'll be no one who's silencing
Earth's joyful sounds of spring,
Replacing winter's quietness
With nature's caroling.

Cloud Creations

Through tattered green-leaf curtaining,
A landscape floats on high.
This beautiful display of white
Is clouds against the sky.

A gang of chubby young-boy clouds
Plays tag or hide and seek.
They get behind their mothers' skirts,
Then lean around to peek.

A regiment of army clouds
Might march on stormy days,
Their guns exploding as they come—
They've bold and frightful ways.

A cloud parade goes passing by,
In front, an elephant,
With many kinds of animals,
And each one different.

A brood of chicken clouds will hop,
Their feathers sticking out.
They're sheltered by the mother hen,
Who leads them all about.

Some cloud teams are adventurers
As they climb out of sight.
They bravely travel everywhere
In sun-bright day or night.

A school of clouds swims slowly by,
Just learning what they're taught.
They have no fear as fishes do
Of ever being caught.

To see such beauty is a gift
From God in His creation.
The cloud formations He has made
Provide us inspiration.

Artist Almighty's Cloud Paintings

What we saw on a mountain drive,
A view that did amaze us,
Some scientists might classify
As cirrus, stratus, nimbus.

Away beyond the cabins that
Sat lonely on the hills
Were clouds of such variety,
Their awesomeness brought chills.

There were so many kinds of shapes
Of different design,
That students of geometry
Could not dare to define.

Light fluffy villages of clouds
In white were pushed away
By tactical invasions of
Some soldier clouds of gray.

Chef Sun placed creamy frosting on
A rich vanilla cake,
Heaped high with many layers on
A gleaming china plate.

With bags of rain, the burdened clouds
Went rolling, racing, gliding.
Suspended by their unseen threads,
They merged without colliding.

A blue sky battled constantly
For places to peek through.
Between the bearded faces,
He made a brave debut.

These scenes of beauty wowed us
And stirred imagination,
This sky show's presentation by
The God of all creation.

Creator's Concert Trio

Heavens, earth, and seas
Were uttered into being
By the majestic voice
Of Lord God Creator.
They play sweet songs together
In three-part harmony,
Directed by God's unseen hand
In glorious performance.
He alone holds the invisible cord
That binds them
Into melody unbroken
In a never-ending concert.
For day's prelude,
The sun awakens
Choruses of birds,
Sheltering in leafy trees,
To sing soaring anthems.
Earth's violins hum
With the teeming life
God has brought forth.
Trees and reeds and goldenrod
Swing and sway together
To the bluesy jazz of the wind.
A tympani of raindrops
Pounds a syncopated rhythm
On earth and seas alike,
Accompanied by booming cymbals
Of heaven's roaring thunder.
At the bidding of the moon,
Sea tides rush in
To swish and swoosh
And crash and slash
Against the silent shores.
Heavens, earth, and seas,
Bound together until the time
Of the Lord's return

With a new heaven and earth,
Follow the arrangement
Of their omnipotent Conductor
In a melodious paean of praise.

Fall Feast

Watermelon, peach, banana, cherry,
Pumpkin, lemon, plum, cranberry,
Apples—golden, red, and green,
Cantaloupe, muscadine, tangerine.

Our Father's fairest feast of all
Is trees fruit-frosted in the fall.

Foretaste

I've been witness to a foretaste
Of God's kingdom's matchless beauty,
In crimson ribbons of sunrise
And gloriously vivid hues
From the Artist's sunset palette.
I've stood, an awed observer of
His magnificent promise,
Embracing all mankind
With streams of color, side by side,
Across a tapestry of endless sky.
I've tasted heaven's nectar
In golden goblets of the sun
And crystal cups of spring rain.
I've heard the voice of the Almighty
In whispers of the wind
And thunder's resonating roar.
I've listened to songs of seeming angel choirs,
Magnifying the Lord of all with hymns.
I've sensed the scents of heaven
In our honeysuckle world.
I've touched the purity of paradise
In a newborn baby's cheek.
Such abundance of wealth on earth,
Provided by our gracious Lord Creator,
Has served as just a preview
Of the riches to someday be enjoyed
In the forever house of my Father.
How blessed am I to be
The daughter of the King!

God's Music

In every morning just at dawn,
God turns His sounds of nature on.
All through the day, His symphony
Plays heaven's music endlessly.

The wind that in the willows sings
Repeats the whir of angels' wings.
As turtledoves commence to coo,
They're seeking sweethearts, soon they'll
    woo.

In summer, swallows, swooping low,
Are humming, crooning as they go.
A choir of birds has varied call;
The mockingbird will trill them all.

The geese go honking as they fly
Across a sullen autumn sky,
And dry leaves, drifting from the trees,
Are rustling with the passing breeze.

In wintertime the sweep of snow
Soft whispers white to land below.
The sleet that pounds with icy ping
Drum rolls staccato with each sting.

As raindrops bring spring flowers cheer,
They turn their heads so they can hear;
Then with the rhythm of romance,
To patter of the rain, they dance.

The gale brings warning, fearsome sound,
Before it hurls the trees around.
The evening storms reverberate
With roaring thunder until late.

The rivers, rushing to the sea,
Create a lilting melody.
The surfs of ocean pound and crash
Repeatedly on shores they lash.

In mating calls, the animals
Compete with sounds of waterfalls
To play their parts instinctively—
No stranger concert could there be.

The bullfrog belts out loud "kerthumps"
To echo when in ponds he jumps.
And then at night the owls ask, "Who?
Who played this program just for you?"

Perhaps God uses a baton
To wave His music off and on
Or claps His hands in accolade
For this recital He has made.

His Survey

Eternal God goes to and fro
Throughout the earth and beyond,
Performing actions from a list
Of deeds omnipotent.
He wakes the sun to rise from sleep
And splinter darkness of the night
With palest pink and lilac beams,
That blaze to boldest orange,
Embroidered with pure gold.
He saturates the sky with clouds,
That shift from shape to shape
And wander place to place
To feed the waiting hungry earth.
He bids white waves depart
From immense blue ocean beds
To pound against vast sandy shores
With the rhythm of His own heartbeat.
He breathes out winds
To cool the burning deserts,
And He exhales fierce and mighty storms
With power that's solely His.
He paints color and hue
From His radiant rainbow palette
To beautify buds and blossoms
And adorn both shrubs and trees
With matchless artistry.
He leads magnificent orchestras
Of winged and feathered beings
In melodic chords of sweetest sounds
To harmonize in hymns of praise
In honor of His greatness.
He manages menageries
Of those in His dominion,
And He oversees affairs of men,
Ever seeking to redeem them.
Then at the end of His survey

Of deeds done for the day,
He stretches out a purple path
For moon and stars to play.
With all His wondrous creativity,
I'm amazed God still has time to see
A sparrow fall . . . and me.

Lady Springtime

With weary Winter's final gasp,
He shuffles off to bed,
And Lady Springtime tiptoes in
To govern in his stead.

Harbinger robin is the first
To note the new arrival
While pecking 'neath the crusty snow
In search of his survival.

The sun's rays are much warmer now
That Lady Springtime's here,
And birds begin to build their nests
And sing sweet songs of cheer.

Soft rains will come to wash away
The last of snow's remains
And soften earth's cracked surfaces
From Winter's icy stains.

The creeks, long frozen, soon will thaw
And burble on their way,
As animals, asleep in dens,
Come out of caves to play.

The trees will don fresh robes again
In varied shades of green,
And leafy shrubs and prickly plants
Will join their verdant scene.

From God's gigantic palette, filled
With every tint and hue,
He'll paint pastel and brilliant buds
To make a grand debut.

The sky's a brighter color here
In Lady Springtime's world
As banner of God's care of earth
In beauty is unfurled.

Nature at Play

In nature's world it's time to play
A game of hide and seek,
When rosebuds rush to hide themselves
And buttercups don't peek.

The monkeys love to play this game.
They run and hide with ease
By climbing to the highest part
Of tall and full-leaved trees.

As bunnies lie behind the shrubs,
The dog with nose in air
Can sense the smell they can't obscure
And chases them from there.

The golden sun might hide behind
Some fleecy clouds of white,
But when they float away from him,
He's left there in plain sight.

Seen frolicking from limb to limb,
The squirrels are having fun,
Pursuing and discovering,
Until the day is done.

The bees conceal themselves inside
A fluffy flower's fuzz.
Although they seem invisible,
One listens for their buzz.

The fish dive down beneath the waves
To search for secret places.
They think they're hid until they're found
By fish teams holding races.

Creation's final crowning gift,
The children, shout with glee,
"Aha, I caught you; now you're it.
You never will find me!"

As God above is looking down
And watching all the while,
I wonder, when He sees His world,
Does it cause Him to smile?

Old Man Winter

When Old Man Winter whistles in
Through autumn's bare-limbed trees,
He tints the blue sky gray again
And instigates a freeze.

He pounds the earth with shards of ice
And stencils in sharp sleet.
With freezing rain he forms a glaze
On every road and street.

He rules the world with gusty winds;
No balmy breezes blow,
For he controls the atmosphere
With crystal tears and snow.

He toils to hide the warmth of sun
And brings night-dark to day.
His chill drives birds to leave their nests
And seek warmth far away.

When people dare to venture out,
Of comfort he disposes.
From rouges in his stiff backpack,
He reddens cheeks and noses.

He sends a shiver to their bones,
Then numbs their hands and feet;
He doesn't stop his torment till
Their misery's complete.

He withers flowers that have dared
To last beyond the fall
With squalls and blizzards He's devised
To decimate them all.

I'm wise to Old Man Winter's plans,
His vengeful aspirations.
I will not let him bother me
With frigid machinations.

He cannot keep from me the glow
Of lamp and fireside,
Nor darken light, where in my heart
My Dear Lord does abide.

Renaissance

When weary Winter walks away,
And Springtime waltzes in,
He leaves his empty cup behind
For her to fill again.

Devoid of color, flower beds
Now rise to the occasion
With brilliant views of varied hues—
A breathtaking sensation.

The mountains cast off soiled white shawls
From all the naked trees,
Where soon will spread toward the sky
Green-coated canopies.

Abandoned playgrounds, parks, and yards,
Once stark and lonely places,
Fill up with laughter, noise, and song,
And happy children's faces.

Dry streams of moisture, long deprived,
Greet April rains with glee,
Then overflow their muddy banks
To rush on merrily.

Tall shrubs that shivered in the cold
Give voice to brittle cries
Till sunshine brings them blossoms sweet
For pastel butterflies.

Farm fallow fields, unoccupied,
Of vegetation bare,
Send forth from early buried seeds,
Fresh plantings everywhere.

To deserts' vacant canvases,
The Painter does arrive
To brush on pink and purple blooms
As rose and cactus thrive.

And I, with hollowness of heart,
To heaven make my plea.
God grants me mercy, grace, and love
From His sufficiency.

Silent Symphony

The flowers all together played
A silent symphony,
Where concert of aromas formed
A splendid potpourri.

The garden was a peaceful site,
A place without dissension,
Until the daffodil complained
She never got attention.

She claimed the rose got too much praise,
And others all agreed.
Each thought the fragrance that she bore
Was just as sweet, indeed.

The honeysuckle boasted that,
With sense olfactory,
She was the instigator used
To stir up memory.

The next to join in the debate,
The summer savory,
Revealed how her rich essence could
Improve a recipe.

The chamomile and lemon balm
Were smug as they could be,
When they shared their importance in
Aromatherapy.

The added voice of hyacinth,
Of plum, of peony,
Of jasmine, of gardenia
Became cacophony.

The sage declared cessation to
This mad buffoonery,
Commanding them to work again
As a perfumery.

She said that God gave everyone
A scent that was unique
To harmonize a bright bouquet
In His outdoor boutique.

Storm at Sea

Seething, foaming, rushing, great majestic ocean
Pounds out wrath relentlessly against all in
      her path.
Once playful waves now reel and roar
To ceaselessly assault the silent shore.

Sullen clouds, like angry hornets, swarm
From out their azure nest
To sting both earth and sea alike
With pummeling, punishing bites.

Lightning shards, as from a giant broken light,
Shatter across the darkening horizon,
While the sun scurries away to hide his golden face
From the fierceness and the fury of the storm.

Thunder shouts with a savage voice
Bass rumblings of his rage,
In tandem with the wailing wind,
Let loose from God's strong hand.

The men at sea in rain-soaked yellow slickers
Attempt to steer their pitching vessels home,
Before their lives are taken as a forfeit
To appease the rising passion of the gale.

Then suddenly, the tempest's put to rest
By the One who calms the wildness of the waters,
And God paints once again across the heavens'
      easel,
The rainbow of His everlasting promise.

Through My Window

Tiny geckos,
Garbed in green,
Brazenly change,
Without a hint
Of modesty,
Into black clothes
To strut
Across my window screen.
Squirrels
In furry gray suits
Stand two legs tall
To show off
White silk shirts.
Papa Cardinal
Takes watchful perch
On bird-feeder roof
While red-headed mama
And babies
Line the ledge
For breakfast.
Little brown wrens
Hide inside
Tall crape myrtle trees
To shake
The tiniest petals
From bright red blossoms.
Petunias,
Gold and purple,
Stand gingerly
On tiptoes
To try to make
Their faces
Touch the sun.
As I watch
This life in nature,
I remember God above

Is ever watching over
Everything I see.

Twilight of the Seasons

'Tis the twilight of the seasons,
When the world winds down for winter,
And the sun makes early curtain
As it ordains night, augmenter.

There's a crispness in the morning.
There's a tingle to the senses.
Only once a year this happens;
It's the magic fall dispenses.

As the green leaves spring had brought forth
Now are dying, they still grasp
From the sun their boldest color
Till they're withered by wind's gasp.

Brilliant blue of sky in summer's
Elbowed out by greedy clouds
That devour smoke from chimneys
And envelop it in shrouds.

Tender flowers sadly shrivel;
All but pansies stay asleep,
Safe beneath the ground till spring comes,
When they've promises to keep.

With the coldness comes migration,
Birds that fly to southern climes.
For the beasts, there's hibernation
Till they welcome warmer times.

While the lakes and ponds are freezing,
Land lies bracing for the snow
To spread wide her crystal blanket
Beyond reach of dull sun's glow.

From the kitchen come aromas,
Apple cake and pumpkin pie—
Here God's human creatures gather,
Thankful for His good supply.

In the Bible there's a reference
To a season for all things,
And I'm partial to this season
For the pleasures autumn brings.

Viola Violet

Viola Violet was so small,
Her tiny stem would bend,
And she would shake with sudden fear
In every blowing wind.

Viola wished that she could hide
When raindrops fell on her.
They were so awful damp and cold,
She was too stiff to stir.

Viola was afraid the sun
Would take away her breath,
Then make her petals all turn brown
And smother her to death.

Viola shook with nervous chills
When winter came with snow.
Her feet were firmly planted, and
She had nowhere to go.

Viola thought the animals
Who scampered all around
Would trample her and stomp on her
And grind her in the ground.

Viola's mother said to her,
"You're quite a scaredy plant.
To be afraid of things so small
As Itsy-Bitsy Ant.

"There is no reason you should live
In constant dread and fear,
For God above created you,
And He is always near.

"God made you to be small, but sweet;
He made you purple, too.
To bring some cheer to cheerless ones
Is what you're meant to do."

Was Summer Made for Barefoot Boys?

Was summer made for barefoot boys
Or barefoot boys for summer?
While some might question which is right,
Boys never stop to wonder.

The shoes that pinch, that bind, that squeeze,
They gladly cast aside,
Preparing winter-tender soles
To toughen like old hide.

They scale up neighbors' apple trees,
Where rough barks bruise their shins,
And apple-sting their friends below,
Who give back sassy grins.

They leap and dance through tingling spray
From Papa's garden hose,
Till ground becomes a slush of mud
To squish between their toes.

The bell that's on the ice cream truck's
Unmatched by siren's song.
They dare to run on sun-scorched streets
For sweetness on the tongue.

They wade through rocky-bottomed creeks
To climb the tallest trestle;
Then, on the softest new-mown grass,
They tumble, roll, and wrestle.

On Mama's cool linoleum,
They tiptoe in for snacks
And never notice when they leave,
Their dusty footprint tracks.

These little lads are seldom still;
Yet, for entire days,
They'll fish upon a river bank,
Despite sun's fiery rays.

God loves these little barefoot boys,
A product of His graces.
Their charm and innocence, He shows
Through smiles on dirty faces.

In Motion by God's Hand

Like little boys, the ocean waves
Are playful coming in.
They toss and tumble, roll and rumble,
All run in a race to win.

With hats hurled high in salty air,
They call to rising sun,
"Come out and play with us today,
We're having so much fun."

Their pockets, filled with gifts they've filched
From ocean's naval stores,
Rich myriads of lovely shells
To give to sandy shores.

They swell and swirl in curve and curl
With patterns never ceasing
Until the time they slide away,
Their hold on land decreasing.

Like crowds of courtly gentlemen,
Who bow with charming manners,
The waves recede in dignity,
Still showing frothy banners.

They ripple, drift, and gently rock,
Move imperceptibly,
To show marine life left behind
They've carried from the sea.

The tides continued rhythmic moves
Are like God's constancy.
I watch His vast creation,
Amazed He thinks of me.

Inspiration

A Gloryland Eternity

Someday I'll get to go to Gloryland
To sing and shout and praise eternally
And march along with saints in heaven's band.

What joy when I my blessed Savior see!
I'll lay my earthly burdens at His feet,
And He will wipe my tears away for me.

The loved ones who have died, I long to meet;
I know that they are waiting for me there.
Reunion time together will be sweet.

With shouts of "Hallelujah" everywhere,
I'll kneel before the holy sinless One
And thank Him for the cross He chose to bear.

I never will have need again for sun
Nor even lamp, for Jesus is the light,
And dark of night will be forever done.

The jeweled walls will be an awesome sight
As I stroll by on streets all made of gold
With Christians from the ages, robed in white,

For just as the apostle had been told,
The church will be arrayed as Jesus' bride,
And I'll be part as prophecy unfolds.

Then endlessly with God will I abide—
No pain nor death in body made anew,
My sins all gone because my Lord had died.

Since every promise in His Word is true,
Someday I'll get to go to Gloryland.
I hope that you are going with me, too.

A Job to Die for

"You are not the right one for this job.
You are not trained and do not have the skill
Or even the experience you need.
Since you lack capability,
You will be sure to fail.
Neither do you have the strength,
The rigor that's required.
You'll risk not just your life,
But also your reputation,
And your family's honor as well.
This position's far too dangerous
For such a lightweight as you.
You're young and immature for this pursuit
And blinded by your own conceit.
What's more, you do not own
The necessary equipment.
You're foolish to think it possible
That you'll achieve success
Where so many others have failed."

Then David picked up five smooth stones,
And taking his sling in his hand,
He approached the giant, Goliath,
The champion of the Philistines,
And in the name of the Lord God Almighty,
He killed him with just one stone.

A Mother's Blessing

The Lord bless you and keep you; the Lord make His face shine upon you, and be gracious to you; the Lord turn his face toward you and give you peace (Numbers 6:24-26).

God bless you, Little Baby Dear,
Here cradled in my arms.
You've captured Daddy's heart and mine,
Enthralled us with your charms.

May God, our Father, keep you near
And cover you with grace,
And may your life reflect His peace
From His own blessed face.

For you created my inmost being; you knit me together in my mother's womb (Psalm 139:13).

The threads God used within my womb,
When He was knitting you,
Had many strands from family
Of past and present, too.

I pray you have your father's strength,
Your mother's tender heart,
And from the generations past,
The best from each a part.

Your eyes saw my unformed body. All the days ordained for me were written in your book before one of them came to be (Psalm 139:16).

God knows what lies ahead for you,
Of happiness your share,
The troubles that may come your way
And sorrows you will bear.

He's written down each day you'll live
Until your days are done.
He did this all before your birth,
Not leaving out a one.

"I know the plans I have for you," declares the Lord, "plans to prosper you and not to harm you, plans to give you hope and a future" (Jeremiah 29:11).

I've no idea what you'll be,
What jobs you will secure,
But in this is my confidence:
God's plans for you are sure.

He'll prosper you and give you hope.
You need have no alarm.
As He's prepared your future,
He has not included harm.

. . . And surely I am with you always, to the very end of the age (Matthew 28:20).

When Jesus came to earth to die
And mankind's sins forgive,
He promised He would be with you
As long as you would live.

And though you're just a wee babe now,
Mere "possibility,"
With God to bless you, you'll become
All He wants you to be.

A Picnic Breakfast

I read how Jesus grilled some fish
Upon a charcoal fire,
Inviting His disciples, "Come and dine."

'Twas on a bank beside the sea,
Where they had fished all night
With not a single fish caught in their nets.

They saw Him standing on the shore
When He called out to them
To let their fishing nets down one more time.

They strained to lift those heavy nets,
Filled now with an abundance,
And as He bade, they brought some fish they'd
      caught.

He questioned Peter of his love
And prophesied his death,
Entreating him to ever "feed My lambs."

The thought of picnic breakfast time,
Prepared by God's own hand,
Caused me to wish I'd been found in their midst.

But as I pondered, I recalled
The picnics where I've been
With Christian friends in blessed fellowship,

When we shared our anticipation of
That "someday" prophesied,
To gather 'round the table with our Lord.

May I be found before that day
With others, who, like Peter,
Display their love by feeding "Jesus' lambs."

A Teacher's Prayer

Lord, help me in my teaching, Your love to demonstrate,
And guide me in my life's work, my service consecrate.
Entrust to me more wisdom for tasks I need to do;
Then grant me greater patience and strengthen me anew.

Forgive me for my sins today; make me forgiving, too.
Help me to think before I speak, and let my words be true.
Revive enthusiasm like I had when I began.
Renew my dedication to do the best I can.

May all my discipline be fair, my class control be good,
And may my students try their best to learn the things they should.
Impart to me the knowledge of words I need to say,
A spirit of discernment to lead my class today.

Empower me with goodness, and make my temper sweet.
May I show only kindness to everyone I meet.
Bless all the students that I teach and guide them, this my prayer.
Then give them happy, useful lives and keep them in Your care.

Before the Beginning of Time

Before the beginning of time, God was,
And His Son was with Him then.

Before the beginning of time, God planned
For a world and all things within.

Before the beginning of time, God knew
That the man he created would sin.

Before the beginning of time, God made
A way to redeem fallen men.

Before the beginning of time, God gave
His Son o'er sin's power to win.

Before the beginning of time, God loved,
And love He has always been.

Brimful of Thanksgiving

Like rivers rise up from their beds
And lakes leap to their banks,
So my soul overflows with praise
And offers God my thanks.

Like sunshine streams across the land
To spill each gilded ray,
Grows my heart rich with gratitude
For mercies new each day.

Like birds begin each morn with song
In joyful harmony,
So sing I then along with them
A grateful melody.

Like bees surround a honey pot,
Where sweetness can be found,
So my soul delves into God's Word,
Where promises abound.

Like all of nature does applaud
Our great Creator's care,
Join I with them in gratefulness
And bow my knees in prayer.

When I reflect upon His love
God gives abundantly,
I'm overwhelmed by what I owe
To Him who died for me.

I Taste the Grace

I taste the grace that's boundless in supply
And feast upon abundant Living Bread.
I've Water from the well that won't run dry.

I pray to be the apple of Your eye.
How sweet each promise from the words You said!
I taste the grace that's boundless in supply.

Help me all evil thoughts and deeds deny;
May I be salt and light for You instead.
I've Water from the well that won't run dry.

Just when I need You most, then You are nigh
If even from Your presence have I fled.
I taste the grace that's boundless in supply.

It's hard to comprehend why You would die,
But for my sins Your precious blood was shed.
I've Water from the well that won't run dry.

Lord, thank you for Your goodness from on high,
Your table that's before me, always spread.
I taste the grace that's boundless in supply.
I've Water from the well that won't run dry.

I Wonder

As she sat among the women
While they did their daily sewing,
Did she sometimes feel the flutter
Of the babe within her growing?

Did she listen to the stories
From the mothers gathered there
Of the pains involved in birthing
And the problems of child care?

Did she often pause to ponder
With her needle in her hand
How it was that she'd been chosen?
Would she ever understand?

Was she fearful for her future?
For this honor she was glad,
But did thoughtless words of others
Find her sometimes feeling sad?

Did she speak to other women
Of the blessing she'd received?
Were there any in this circle
Who knew truth that she believed?

Was she trusting that her Man-child
Who was promised as a King
Would become o'er sin the victor
And the world salvation bring?

Did her faithful heart within her
Meet with God in sweet accord
As she sat in prayerful waiting,
Making garments for the Lord?

Keep Me in the Center of Your Will

Keep me in the center of Your will today.
Help me say the words that You would have me say.
Guide me as I travel all along the way.
Keep me in the center of your will

When there is a deed of kindness I should do,
When there is a task I need to carry through,
When I need forgiveness, help me come to you.
Keep me in the center of Your will.

Teach me of the love and patience I must know.
Help me in the knowledge of Your Word to grow.
Let my life the grace of God to others show.
Keep me in the center of Your will.

In Your will, Lord, let me be,
In Your perfect place for me.
In Your will, Lord, let me stay.
I would live for You, today.

Life's Blowouts

And just like that—the tire blew;
Disaster was awaiting you.
Your life has blowouts when you chance
An unexpected circumstance:

The friend who knew your heart betrayed
The spouse you pledged your life to strayed
The babe you longed for was stillborn
For life that might have been, you mourn
A tragic illness diagnosed
The unrelenting pain you host
The sudden loss of one held dear
You can't believe she's not still here
Your children, holding all your dreams
Sidetracked by Satan's evil schemes
Imprisoned for a traitor's lie
By judge whose justice went awry
The fire, the floods, the raging wind
Your home destructs and all within
The job lost you had worked life-long
The money you had saved all gone
The plans you had created, crashed
The goals you'd set your heart on, smashed.

Take heart, my friends, your God is near.
There's not a prayer He does not hear.
There's not a single tragedy
That His all-seeing eye can't see.

His love's like none you can compare;
Your every pain and loss, He'll share.
With Him there is no hopelessness;
In perfect peace, your heart can rest.

Morning Prayer

Before the sun climbs to her perch, announcing each
    new day
With pinks and purples o'er the sky, I bow my head to
    pray.

*Lord, thank You for your awesome works, Your
    beauty in creation.*
*Each panorama that You paint is cause for
    inspiration.*

*I praise You for Your steadfast love, salvation, full and
    free,*
*For mercies new each morning, and grace You grant
    to me.*

*You've blessed me so abundantly, supplied my every
    need,*
And even in the trying times, I know You'll safely lead.

*I'm thankful for Your oversight of all things
    everywhere,*
*And that You always listen when I come to You in
    prayer.*

I ask for Your protective hand on friends and family,
*That You will guide and safely keep the ones so dear to
    me.*

*Deliver them from Satan's ploys and draw them close
    to You;*
*Then shelter them beneath Your wings and make them
    strong and true.*

*And, Father, would You bless Your church around the
    world today?*

May Gospel reach to hungry hearts, both near and far away.

Please help our nation's leadership to listen to Your voice.
When You divine direction give, may they make that their choice.

Direct our country to return to values of the past,
When founded on your Holy Word with virtues that would last.

And with armed service personnel, I pray that you'll abide.
May firemen and policemen feel your presence at their sides.

For those with needs of every kind, I ask Your healing touch,
As well as any in distress who need your help so much.

May I work for Your kingdom's good until You come again,
My life bring honor to Your name, for Jesus' sake, Amen.

Then when the moon has scaled the heights to end the realm of sun,
I'll kneel in meditation to thank God for all He's done.

Praise Abounding

The morning sun awakens to announce that day is here.
God's in control of everything; we have no need to fear.

The rivers and the waterfalls race lakes down to the sea,
Declaring as they rush along, God's might and majesty.

While rustling, the leaves praise God with whispers from the wind.
To laud their great Creator's skill, the trees in honor bend.

The flowers breathe out sweet perfume to worship in their way
With colors, bold and beautiful, in wonderful array.

The mountains also do their part to make God's presence known.
Through lofty peaks of loveliness, His grandeur there is shown.

The sunset introduces night in gold-touched pinks and blues,
Presenting handiwork of God in awesome pastel hues.

The firmament of stars reveals that God is over all.
He never falters, never fails; He hears us when we call.

The hosts of angels magnify the greatness of God's name,
With "Hallelujah to the King! He's holy!" they proclaim.

The ministers in pulpits preach that we can be sin-free,
For Jesus died upon the cross and rose in victory.

The ones who teach in Sunday School tell stories of
    God's love,
So little ones can learn the truth of Him who dwells
    above.

The Christian neighbor takes a meal to someone who's
    in need.
She represents the hands of God with hungry souls to
    feed.

The missionaries give the news: Salvation's from the
    Lord.
They share the Gospel's wondrous words: In heaven
    there's reward.

The Bible tells us of God's plan that we might realize:
The role of nature, angels, man is to evangelize.

Rare Gems of Recollection

In moments held in retrospect,
Pluck from your mine of memory
The rare gems you can recollect.

Look back on days without defect
When things were all as they should be,
In moments held in retrospect.

Remember how God did protect
When danger dogged you suddenly,
The rare gems you can recollect,

Supernal strength that He'd inject
When your strength was illusory,
In moments held in retrospect.

Hold fast to what you'd not expect—
A sad day ending blissfully,
The rare gems you can recollect.

Recall when you would not elect
To harm with words an enemy,
In moments held in retrospect.

Consider and reserve respect
For an amazing victory,
The rare gems you can recollect.

See how the brightness can reflect
The jewels in heart's treasury,
In moments held in retrospect,

Those memories that you dissect
When blue moon was accessory,
The rare gems you can recollect.

Viewed all together, you'll detect
The proof of God's abundancy,
In moments held in retrospect,
The rare gems you can recollect.

Road to Paradise

"Are we there yet?"
Asks the traveler.

"Not yet, my child.
The road ahead is very long,
With mountains to climb,
Rivers to ford,
And valleys to travel through.
You'll rest in pleasant fields
With amiable companions
And dance to music
Only you can hear
As you journey along.
You'll pass through storms
Where strong winds blow,
And you'll trip in rough places and fall,
But when your strength will waver,
It is then I'll carry you.
When what's before you is obscured
By fog or darkest night,
And you can't find your direction,
I'll guide you with my hand
Upon your shoulder.
You'll gather bouquets of roses,
Feeling petals of velvet
And breathing in sweetest perfume,
Not noticing the thorns
Until they pierce you.
With pebbles in your shoes
And rainbows overhead,
You'll stride along with purpose
To reach your destination
In the days of your wayfaring.
If you keep looking straight ahead,
Neither turning aside for bright lights
Nor being deterred by savage beasts,

You will not lose your way.
As you sojourn on this road,
Just follow the signs I've given
To reach the other side.
My gate is open wide,
And the price for you to enter has been paid
For an eternity with me in Paradise."

Simon's Soliloquy

In borrowed tomb, they laid Him,
My Master, yesterday.
My hope has died with Jesus' death,
My Light of joy, extinguished.
The bleakness of this twilight hour
Brings darkness to my soul.

No one, but He, had understood
My brash impulsiveness
Nor loved me quite so dearly.
What wretched man denied Him in
His hour of sorest need?
'Twas I—Oh, God, forgive me.

My hope has died with Jesus' death,
My Light of joy, extinguished.
I'd glanced just once at Mary near the cross,
Her shoulders, bent with pain,
As if the sword that pierced His side
Had pierced her flesh as well.

So many blessed hours now, I hold in memory.
While sitting at His feet to hear Him speak,
I learned the truths He wanted all to know.
I see the happy faces still
Of lame He made to walk and blind He made to see
And families of loved ones He had healed.

I treasure moments I recall,
Like when I walked on water.
I would not have been sinking,
Had I kept my eyes on Him.
And once the very Son of God
Did kneel and wash my feet.

He changed my name to Peter, meaning rock;
He said that He would build His church on me.
I've wondered what He meant when He said that.
Nor did I understand His words to Jews,
That if the temple were to be torn down,
In three days, He'd restore it once again.

I'll never comprehend the love
He showed to everyone,
To lonely ones, the sad, and sinners all,
To Judas who betrayed Him, or to those
Who had Him beaten cruelly
And later put to death upon the cross.

Where can we go from here?
Our Teacher, Master, Lord
Has gone from us for good,
And now we have no one whom we can follow.
My hope has died with Jesus' death,
My Light of joy, extinguished.

* * *

In twenty-four short hours,
My world has turned around.
The darkness of the twilight hour
Cannot invade my soul.
All glory be to our great God;
His Son is resurrected.

When first I heard He'd risen,
I could not believe it true;
I ran to see the tomb where He had lain.
When He appeared among us,
Where we'd hidden from the Jews,
I could have leaped and shouted out for joy.

He showed us where His wounds had been
And helped us understand His prophecies.

He breathed on us His living Holy Spirit,
Then sent us out to share life in His name.
My hope has been revived with His return;
My Light of joy's alive forevermore.

Surety

When I'm not sure what path to choose
And which direction to refuse

When I can't see what lies concealed
And wait for truth to be revealed

When problems occupy my mind,
And sweet release I cannot find

When troubles seem to linger near,
And all I do is fret and fear

When I'm bewildered and bemused,
And all my thoughts become confused

When straight ahead, the way is blurred
And not a voice of hope is heard

* * *

Those times I do not hesitate
Upon God's Word to meditate.

Then humbly, I, before Him kneel
And feel His presence, close and real.

I offer up my earnest prayers
And cast on Him my deepest cares.

Then, when I cannot see His face,
I'll trust in His enduring grace.

I know His promises are true;
Each day He'll surely see me through.

Though difficulties lie ahead,
By His strong hand will I be led.

That All May Know

I AM PERSUADED . . .
By the sun, keeper of the day
Rising with each dawn to make the darkness light
And sinking in gold and orange glory at day's end
And by the moon, watchman of the night
Who echoes the sun with his paler imitation
By brilliant stars, too numerous to count
Dancing an ode of joy in the firmament

By raging rivers that rush to the seas
Which teem with myriads of aquatic life
By billows of clouds, racing to and fro
To replenish the earth with rain
And by torrential storms, ravaging the land
Along with what man has assembled

By flawless formations of traveling geese
Sailing across an endless sea of sky
And by Lilliputian hummingbirds
Sipping sustenance from fragrant blossoms
By the feral beauty of the tiger
Fearlessly foraging for prey
And by diminutive armies of ants
Diligently constructing intricate colonies

By a proliferation of exquisite flowers
Seasoning the world with color and aroma
And by the vastness of the universe
Yet to be fully explored by curious mankind
By massive mountains
Wreathed with regal robes of green
And by craggy canyons
Slipping into the depths of the earth

By the miracle of new life
Formed by an unseen hand

In deepest recesses of the waiting womb
And by the instinctive nature
Of a mother to nurture her young
By the yearning of the human heart
To bow in worship to the One
Who is Creator of all things
... THAT GOD IS.

This I Believe

That winter's raucous roar
Will be swallowed up
By the gentle whisper of spring

That the sun will rise
On each new day
To warm the earth below

That moon and stars
Will keep their place
In night sky's firmament

That clouds will go forth
Without end
To seed the earth with rain

That tender bulbs
Buried deep within the ground
Will one day lift their heads in glorious bloom

That trees which stand in winter
Trembling naked in the cold
Will dress in vibrant green again

That God's love like a candle
Standing tall within our hearts
Burns with an everlasting flame

That every promise in God's Word
Is absolutely true
In Him we can safely put our trust

That the sorrows suffered here on earth
Will all be gone forever
In God's eternity

That loved ones
Who have gone before
Will meet us in joyful reunion

That our Savior's death and resurrection
Giving meaning for this life
Are the only hope of heaven

Your God Has Not Forsaken You

Oppressed by the problems around you?
Confused by the cares that confound you?
Concerned for what the future holds?
Afraid to watch as it unfolds?
Your God has not forsaken you.

God's covenant will be with you.
His promises are ever true.
Compassionately He forgives.
His everlasting love He gives.
Your God has not forsaken you.

Fear not the tricks of evil schemer.
The Lord of Hosts is your Redeemer.
His heritage is your increase.
Accept with joy His promised peace.
Your God has not forsaken you.

Just for Fun

A Baptized Cat

"Here, Kitty Kitty," called the child,
While looking all around,
But Kitty was suspicious and
Was nowhere to be found.

"Now where could that old cat have gone?"
His little mistress said.
"I bet he's hiding somewhere near,
Like underneath my bed.

"Aha, I found you, Silly Cat,"
She laughed and gave a shout,
As on her knees beside her bed,
She dragged the kitten out.

Then quietly she tiptoed to
The bathroom in the hall,
Where earnestly she told her pet,
"This won't hurt you at all."

Then making sure the door was closed,
She turned toward the sink,
And filling it with water said,
"It's not for you to drink."

She'd seen baptisms at her church,
When people testified
To how much joy salvation brought
And peace they had inside.

She asked her cat, "Have you been saved?"
And looked him in the eye,
"And will you live your life for Christ
Till He comes by and by?

"I'll baptize you, dear Brother Cat,
In Jesus' holy name;
Like Preacher did it at the church,
I'm doing it the same."

At that, she pushed him in the sink
And tried to hold him tight,
But Kitty gave a mighty leap
And landed out of sight.

She found him crouched beside the tub
With terror in his eyes,
Then went to get her baby doll,
Another to baptize.

A Feast of Manuscripts

In offices of editors
Are manuscripts galore.
Lepisma Saccharina love
These readings to explore.

"Hooray!" cries Sybil Silverfish
To all her family.
"I've found a pile of papers here.
How lucky could we be!"

"Just what I'd hoped to see," says Cy,
"Collected recipes.
I bet I'll find a cake and pie.
Sweet treats are sure to please."

"Although the words seem alien,
And that does not surprise,
Sci-fi's most suited to my taste,"
Sylvester shyly sighs.

"Look, here's a book of prayers," says Sid,
A smile upon his face.
"I never thought I'd have a chance
To be consuming grace."

"I'm nibbling on politics;
I can't imagine why,"
Sabrina states disgustedly.
"The pages are so dry."

"I'm mad for music," Cyrus says,
"What joy this songbook brings!"
Between each mouthful he enjoys,
He rapturously sings.

"Philosophy's my cup of tea
With wise words from the sages."
Sinclair proclaims how he enjoys
The wisdom of the ages.

"I'm savoring such rich romance,"
Sophia rhapsodizes.
"Too much of that will make you sick."
Celina then advises.

Says Cicero, the connoisseur,
"I've tasted for a test,
Some travel and some history,
But poetry tastes best.

The author of these manuscripts
They'd labored long to write
Will likely never even know
We feasted here tonight."

A Tincture of Writer's Craft

While shopping in the stationer's,
I saw exotic inks,
And right beside them was a shelf
Of writers' favorite drinks.

A single bottle drew my eye;
I thought I'd like to try it.
Before another grabbed it first,
I stepped right up to buy it.

The drink was labeled "Writer's Craft,"
The skill of my desire.
I hoped that by imbibing, I'd
Dexterity acquire.

When I got home, I popped the cork
And took a couple sips.
My talent started rising as
The first taste crossed my lips.

My muse, that I'd not seen for months,
Came out of hiding boldly,
Apologizing he'd of late
Been treating me so coldly.

We sat together, he and I,
While I consumed my potion.
And then he jumped into my mind
And set my hands in motion.

I typed some lines of words so fast
With such facility,
I gazed with great amazement at
My strange ability.

Though Shakespeare was a genius,
A literary artist,
Of all the world's word artisans,
I must now be the smartest.

But my elixir soon wore off.
Alas! My muse departed,
And I was left with naught to write—
Alone and broken-hearted.

Can You Feel My Pain

I might be just a bit fanatical
For language that is ungrammatical.
It hurts my ears; indeed, that's factual.
The pain I feel is truly actual.

For verb tense that has gone awry,
I'm seized by pangs and almost cry.
"I seen him when he took a fall;
I wish he hadn't fell at all."

For pronoun errors I must brace.
"This here—that there," I cannot face.
With "Me and her will go," I sigh.
I wince to hear "for you and I."

A double negative can make
My eardrums and my head to ache.
Words "I ain't got nobody's" sad.
And even when they're sung, they're bad.

When subjects don't with verbs agree,
The poor construction pierces me.
"Here is two apples"—how that bites!
And "It don't matter" smarts by rights.

When grammar rules are thus abused,
I'm in distress for how they're used.
I cannot help my strong reaction;
I utter "Ow!" for each infraction.

A Touch of Gold

Awaking from a purple dream,
I found the world had changed.
The whole outdoors was yellow now
With colors rearranged.
The flowers, one-time rainbow-like,
Had each been tinted yellow.
I thought just buds and petals were,
But it was hard to tell though.
The leaves and limbs and trunks of trees
All had a yellow cast.
I couldn't help but wonder how
This coloring could last.
The grass, although not withering,
Had turned a different shade,
With brilliant yellow highlighting
On every single blade.
There were no black or brown or white,
Just only yellow dogs.
The strangest sight of all to me
Was once-green yellow frogs.
The pigs, the cows, the barnyard cat—
Each wore a yellow hat.
The roosters' combs were yellow, too.
Can you imagine that?
In lemon-yellow woolly coats
Were little newborn lambs,
Attired like their Mama ewes,
As well as Papa rams.
The sky was yellow, odd indeed,
A gleaming gold horizon,
A scene to me as awesome as
I'd ever laid my eyes on.
The mountains had a yellow glow;
The oceans had one, too.
And as I saw the world transformed,
Amazement grew and grew,

Until I saw the brilliant sun
With shining yellow rays
Had put a glow on all outside
In Great Creator's praise.

Come Go with Me to Join the Cloud Parade

Come go with me to join the cloud parade.
We'll climb up high to heaven's soaring show.
You'll hold my hand, and I won't be afraid.
Such sights we'll see in our grand promenade,
Beneath us all of earth spread out below.
Come go with me to join the cloud parade.
In fleecy robes of white, we'll be arrayed.
We'll watch the changing seasons as we go.
You'll hold my hand, and I won't be afraid.
We'll march across the sky with brass brigade,
Our weapons only raindrops to bestow.
Come go with me to join the cloud parade.
When evening comes and light begins to fade,
We'll wander through the darkness to and fro.
You'll hold my hand, and I won't be afraid.
Suspended in our shifting colonnade,
When sun arrives again, we'll be aglow.
Come go with me to join the cloud parade.
You'll hold my hand, and I won't be afraid.

Fowl Play

Hear the story of Young Chelsea Chicken
As she pecked out her place in the world.
What her mother observed in the henhouse
Got her temper and feathers unfurled.

She said, "Chelsea, watch out for those "cluckers."
They will bring your good name to disgrace.
If you fly with such chicks in the future,
You will end up with egg on your face.

If you follow those biddies too closely,
They will lead you across the wrong road,
Where you'll lie in the ditch without cover,
And you'll reap the wild seeds that you sowed.

You must not fly the coop with those bad birds;
Their activities you must refuse,
Since we're branded as birds of a feather
By the kinds of companions we choose.

So before you become chicken salad,
Just remember how our name was made,
When the Lord used the crow of a rooster
To show Peter his Lord he'd betrayed.

It's our part to scratch out our existence,
And be willing to do what it takes.
Though it's true that we can't soar like eagles,
Then, at least, we don't crawl like the snakes.

Don't let yourself be chicken-hearted.
Do not squawk about what's on your plate.
Don't forget that the God of all nature
Is in charge of each creation's fate."

Francina's Green Fever

Francina Frog was feeling sick,
Though no one would believe her.
She said she'd been infected by
A bad case of green fever.

The winter doldrums had set in
Through drab and dreary days,
Where all she'd seen surrounding her
Were browns and dingy grays.

And then, as though a wand were waved
With magic "hocus pocus,"
She saw some sprigs were springing up
From bulbs of budding crocus.

Forsythia and daffodils
Gave puny stems a push,
Before the foliage could grow out
On rose and snowball bush.

At sight of trees unfurling leaves,
Her bug eyes bugged out more
At ash and aspen, sassafras,
Beech, birch, and sycamore.

And when new blades of grass appeared,
Francina was elated.
She shouted from her lily pad,
"My fever has abated."

Her fever gone, she sang this song
In bass cacophony,
Amid some most gigantic jumps,
"The whole world looks like me!"

Handout Hodgepodge

You need any? I have many—handouts
To make your English scholars standouts.

Every Kind of Sentence Part
E.A. Poe's "The Tell-Tale Heart"
What to Know for Punctuation
Ways to Write a Good Summation
Grammar Rules to Memorize
How to Edit and Revise
Pronouns and Their Antecedents
Essay Topics—Thesis Statements
Novels, Poems, Biographies
Metaphors and Similes
Quotes from William Shakespeare's Plays
How to Tell a Clause from Phrase
Spelling and Vocabulary
Criticism Literary
Limericks to Bring You Laughs
Writing Decent Paragraphs
Wit, Satire, and Parody
Knighthood's Days of Chivalry
Legend, Epic, Allegory
How to Write a Good Short Story
Alliteration, Rhythm, Rhyme
Verb Tenses in the Present Time
Connotation—Denotation
Caesar's Funeral's Oration
Aphorism—Apostrophe
All Forms of the Verb "To Be"
Your or You're and There, Their, They're
Nouns—A Usage Questionnaire
Keep a Journal ; Keep a Log
Sandburg's Little Poem "Fog"
Oxymorons—Paradoxes
Fable of the Grapes and Foxes

I made these for my class to use,
But they said handouts give them blues.

It's a Crime

Outside the little country church
Stood Maudie with her friends,
Old ladies, clucking round her like
A gossiping of hens.

"I think it's just a crime," she sighed,
"That Kathryn's in the choir.
The ones who get the punishment
Are those who stand beside her.

She sounds just like an old foghorn,
Directing ships to shore,
Except her voice is so off-key,
There's none would seek to moor.

The congregation's punished, too,
By her discordant voice.
They'd like to see her gone, I'm sure,
Were they to have the choice."

The ladies nodded their assent,
Four bobbing heads of gray.
There wasn't one who'd disagree,
With what she'd had to say.

Then round the corner came a lass,
Of maybe six or seven.
"You better change your ways," said she,
"Or you won't go to heaven.

"For what you said 'bout my grandma,
That seems to me a crime,
And you'll be punished 'you know where'
For all the rest of time."

She flounced away, and Maudie said,
"The truth is never wrong.
I do not lie; it is a crime
How Kathryn sings a song."

For Maudie would not change her heart,
Her criticizing Spirit,
She kept on putting others down
To all who liked to hear it.

Jealousy Is for the Birds

"Have you noticed," chirped a sparrow from her nest,
"How outlandishly the goldfinch female's dressed?"

Sighed her mate from perch up higher in the tree,
"What she's wearing doesn't matter much to me."

Said she, "The male must think that he's a prize;
To see such brilliant color hurts my eyes."

She tweeted on how gaudy they appear,
Not sensing there might be a goldfinch near.

Although her mate grew tired of her tirade,
With words of comfort, wisdom he displayed:

"While our appearance may not cause sensation,
We're still a vital part of God's creation.

God said that not a one of us would fall,
But He would be nearby to see it all.

Your gray and brown are beautiful to me,
And not another sings as prettily."

At that, she fluttered down to gather seed
For hungry babies in the nest to feed.

A goldfinch, never pausing in his flight,
Bestowed upon her head a crown of white.

Miranda Ant

Miranda Ant had slept all day
Which made the others mad.
Said Andrew Ant, "I'm 'shamed of you;
Your laziness is sad."

Amanda Ant derided her
About the tasks she'd shirk.
She said, "It's up to all of us
When it comes time to work."

Said Randy Ant in deep disgust,
"This one thing I believe,
If you were queen, you'd lay no eggs
For workers to receive."

And Clancy Ant then spoke his piece
And nudged her with his knee,
"Get up and help me shove this rock;
It's way too big for me."

When Daniel Ant saw her abed,
He couldn't understand
Why she was not out pushing dirt
Beneath the bulging land.

Then Nancy Ant came next to her
And yelled right in her ear,
"If you're not up within the hour,
I'll stomp you—do you hear?"

Then Brandon Ant tried kinder words,
"You know we love you, Dear,
But when the sun is in the sky,
It's our job to appear."

He added in his speech to her,
"I do not want to fuss,
But to remind you for our ways
The Bible praises us.

Samantha Ant then had a plan
To find a picnic place.
She knew Miranda loved them and
Would surely show her face.

And then Cassandra Ant came close
To shoo them all away.
"Can you not tell she's dead?" she said,
"And been that way all day?"

Monologue of the Merciless Editor

"Oh me, oh my!" said the editor.
"Correcting this is quite the chore.

Is this the best that you can muster?
This story's totally lackluster.

The writing is so uninspired;
Just reading through it makes me tired.

It's my job to inform you that
Your characters are cardboard-flat.

Their dialogue is somewhat static,
Their interaction, problematic.

And can't you tell this phrase is wrong?
It's hackneyed as a country song.

The verbs you've used are lacking action;
Your adjectives are pure distraction.

Descriptions here are not poetic;
I'd say that they're downright pathetic.

Your plot line wanders round and round.
No resolution can be found.

Your thoughts are not original.
I see no spark of life at all.

I'm trying here to be polite,
But I insist that you rewrite.

In fact, I have a better plan:
Throw this away—begin again."

*For criticism that's dispersed,
My inner editor's the worst.*

Muse Lost in the Library

I took my muse to the library
One dreary rainy day,
And when I turned to look for him,
I found he'd run away.

I searched for him in the travel books,
No telling where he'd be—
In mountains, beaches, wilderness,
Somewhere across the sea.

Adventure stories I saw next,
A special draw for him.
Though many heroes tarried there,
He wasn't one of them.

I browsed amid tomes classical
And strolled through poetry,
And while verse was his favorite,
He wasn't there for me.

I looked through shelves of how-to books,
My first choice: how to write,
And though that's where I thought he'd be,
Not one glimpse did I sight.

To track him down, I ventured forth
And even took a chance,
I rushed through math and science books
And lingered in romance.

In volumes inspirational,
I circled round and round,
Then reasoned if he wasn't here,
He was not to be found.

I'd gone through Dewey Decimal,
Done everything but shout.
Not finding hide nor hair of him,
I guessed that he'd checked out.

I really miss him since he's gone;
Without him I'm no good.
I'd keep him chained up by my side
If there's a way I could.

Ohhh . . . It Hurts Just Thinking about It

I can't believe I ate all that—
Just filled with calories and fat.

With onion rings did I begin
And spicy sauce to dip them in.

My fresh green salad, I'm confessing,
Had croutons crowned with blue cheese dressing.

Of chicken soup, I had a bowl,
As well as soft white dinner roll.

With pork ribs, honey barbecued,
Were apples with brown sugar stewed.

The French fries were a crisp delight,
Their cheddar topping, "outta sight."

I ate no green beans, corn, or peas,
Sans salt, sans seasoning, sans cheese.

But there were vegetables sautéed,
In cream and butter, I'm afraid.

Dessert time I just had to try
Both cheesecake and some pecan pie.

I topped it all with almond coffee
And caramel and chocolate toffee.

Ohhh, how I had a stomach ache . . .
Till suddenly did I awake.

I'd dreamed my dinner, rich foods packed,
My diet started, still intact.

Such a Fuss about Nothing

My teacher pitches quite a fit
When I won't do my work.
It's really not that big a deal,
But still, she goes berserk.

She says we can't chew bubble gum.
That's such a silly rule,
And when I chew it anyway,
She loses all her cool.

When I am late to class, she acts
Like that's a major crime.
It's just a couple minutes, but
It gets her every time.

When I start mocking when she speaks,
She thinks that I'm a jerk.
Her face gets red all over, while
I just sit there and smirk.

She has no patience, none at all.
I think it's kind of odd,
The way she lost her mind because
I'd spit a paper wad.

She really blew a gasket once,
The time I punched a kid.
When I play with my buddies is
No cause to blow her lid.

She didn't like it one small bit—
That tack upon her chair.
She had no sense of humor when
She sat right on it there.

She wrote a letter to my mom
That said I'm a distraction.
Each tiny thing that I had done,
She called a rule infraction.

If I became the teacher here,
My classes would be fun.
I'd never make nitpicky rules
Or fuss at anyone.

The Fool Has Said in His Heart

Some moles, while working underground,
Decreed, "There is no sun."
For this pronouncement, they made signs
To share with everyone.

Inside the woods, an elephant,
Who saw the signs, concluded,
"The murkiness beneath the trees
Just proves a sun's excluded."

The owl, who squinted at the signs
Beneath the moon's diffusion,
Averred believers of the sun
Were suffering delusion.

A little bear, inside a cave
For winter's hibernation,
Concurred with words upon the sign,
Expressing some frustration.

An ostrich, told about the signs,
Accorded they were right.
His head was buried in the sand;
He couldn't see the light.

The rabbits in their hutches and
The squirrels in leafy trees
Declared the signs a sentiment
With which they could agree.

The lion, though he saw the sun,
Put forth his point of view.
"If I can't touch it, it's not real;
I say the signs are true."

The sun awakened with the dawn,
Alive with colors richly drawn.
The sun awakened with the dawn,
Ignored the signs, and shone right on.

Won't You Have a Cookie?

The Christmas season's time to bake,
And cookies are such fun to make—
Rolled or kneaded, pressed in bars,
Dropped or shaped like trees and stars,
Topped with Christmas-colored sprinkles,
Fringed in tiny candy crinkles.

I have to go to great expense
To get the best ingredients:
Sugar, butter, eggs, and milk,
Flour sifted soft as silk,
Pumpkin, ginger, fresh strawberries,
Oatmeal, raisins, red ripe cherries,
Blocks of chocolate, semi-sweet,
Crushed pineapple, glazed mincemeat,
Fruit that's dried and fruit that's not,
Lemon, fig, and apricot,

Chopped pecans and walnut pieces,
Peanut butter cups from Reese's,
Vanilla, cocoa, peppermint
To yield a lovely, tempting scent,
Cinnamon and orange spice
For more aromas that are nice,
And butterscotch or Hershey's kisses,
Making sweet treats more delicious.

So many cookie specialties,
Like coffee-flavored biscottis,
Scottish shortbread, snickerdoodles,
Layered logs with Chinese noodles,
Pinwheels, wafers, snaps, and tarts,
Snowballs, sandies, jellied hearts,
Crisp or crunchy, soft or chewy,
Frostings firm and icings gooey.

I place the dough on cookie sheet
In oven turned on to preheat,
Then cool on counter when they're done.
And offer some to everyone.

Won't you have a cookie?

Gabby Groceries

As I walked through the grocery,
Some items spoke to me.
A peach said, "Please don't touch me there.
I've bruises; can't you see?"

A steak told me his grade was "A"
As though that might impress.
I wondered who his teacher was.
He'd passed a test, I guess.

Two soup cans hollered out to me
As I strolled by their shelf.
One said, "My label's prettier,
If I say so myself."

The other simply heaved a sigh,
"I'll match him, ounce for ounce.
His contents are deplorable.
It's what's inside that counts."

When I surveyed a row of brooms,
One asked me for a dance,
And if I'd been there all alone,
He might have stood a chance.

I gazed at fresh baked pies and cakes,
Just savoring the smell,
But not a one had words for me.
I'm sure that's just as well.

You may think I was dreaming here,
But all of this is true.
My groceries do talk to me.
Don't yours converse with you?

You do not have to be asleep
To hear their conversation,
Just wide awake and listening
With your imagination.

Bossy Bird

A bird that no one else can see
Goes everywhere along with me.
He perches lightly on my sleeve;
I surely wish that he would leave!

He thinks that he's a diet guru
And tries to tell me what I should do.
Sometimes I hear him softly mutter,
"Eat biscuits dry; you don't need butter.
In fact, you really don't need bread;
Just eat some carrot sticks instead."
I wish he'd go and soak his head.

I have a sweet tooth that's so healthy,
If it were money, I'd be wealthy.
I like cookies, cakes, and pies,
And if I eat them, he just sighs.
He knows I'm fond of chocolate;
I mean I love it—quite a lot!
He thinks I'll give it up—or not!

I also like ice cream and candy;
The both of them are fine and dandy,
But he's a killjoy—that's for sure.
For all those things with such allure,
Like sweets and like potato chips,
He says that when they pass my lips,
They'll rest forever on my hips.

A bird that no one else can see
Goes everywhere along with me.
He perches lightly on my sleeve;
I surely wish that he would leave.

Reflections

A Family Christmas

At Christmas time my heart returns
On wings of memory
To home, when I was just a girl
And there with family.

The times were simpler in those days,
And we had modest means,
But in my mind's eye I recall
The happiest of scenes.

The scents of baking in the air
And decorated tree
Were beacons to my brothers, to
My sister, and to me.

The carols that my mother sang
Still echo in my ears.
Her sweet soprano's just as clear,
Though it's been many years.

The Christmas dinner Mom prepared
Was great in every way,
And all those tasty treats she made
I wish I had today.

My father at this season was
The most excited one.
The joyfulness he found in life
Made holidays more fun.

His tender nature made our home
A blessed place to be.
The love he showed to all of us
Made God's love plain to see.

Now Mom and Dad are home in heaven,
And though I don't know when,
I've hopes that all my loved ones will
Have Christmas there with them.

Leon's Story

Wee, tow-headed lad,
Dressed in Sunday suit
And bowler hat just like Daddy's,
Sat on the porch
To pose for the camera.
At Mama's urging,
He offered a shy smile.
Sprawled beside him was
His companion in mischief,
A white dog of dubious parentage
With a black patch over one eye.
The very second that
Picture taking was over,
The lad rushed inside.
Pulling off shoes, socks, suit,
He changed into old clothes,
Then raced on chubby bare feet
To play in the backyard.
On his way out,
He picked up a broom,
Which he proceeded to swing
Round and round
While he ran in circles.
In a chair beside him,
Mama sat snapping green beans.
She warned him to watch out
For the dog.
As he continued to turn
In a dizzy fashion,
His dog yipping around him,
He suddenly hit it
Square in the head.
When the dog fell over unconscious,
Mama said, "Son, I believe
You've killed your dog."
It was many long minutes

Before the dog stirred,
And the little lad, grown,
Still smiles when he tells this story.

An Embarrassment of Blessings

Oh, Father in Heaven,
How could it be,
That I, so undeserving,
Receive from Your gracious hand
An embarrassment of blessings?

Beauty of Your creation,
Spread before me,
Like a never-ending banquet,
Sunrise and sunset,
A most magnificent feast,
With brightest sunshine, freshest rain
To nourish and sustain me.

Your forgiveness of my sins,
Those remembered
And those I have forgotten,
A soothing salve
Upon my wounded soul,
Your comfort in distress and pain,
A shawl of warmth
Wrapped around my heart.

Dear family and friends,
A lamp to shine
Against my loneliness,
But, most of all,
The Son of God,
My never-failing Friend,
Whoever walks beside me
And illuminates my path.

Your precious Holy Word,
My guide for each new day—
Your promises, the bridge of hope
I'll walk across to glory

To sit and learn at Jesus' feet,
As His disciples did,
And rise to sing Hosannas
With all the saints and angels.

This is too much for me to comprehend.
I thank You, Lord.

And God Smiled

When first we met, we did not know
How different we were.
We only knew we were in love;
On that we did concur,
And God smiled.

While he liked best the winter days,
I couldn't wait for spring,
When flowers stretched to reach the sun,
And birds began to sing,
And God smiled.

We married on a summer night
With heat somewhat oppressive.
I really didn't mind it, but
He found it quite depressive,
And God smiled.

Although I served his dinners warm,
He sometimes coolly spurned them.
While learning how to be a cook,
Quite often I had burned them,
And God smiled.

Two children came to bless our home
And add a new dimension.
We didn't note the temperature;
They took all our attention,
And God smiled.

Then with the children grown and gone,
We played a little game.
The thermostat that he'd turn down,
I'd turn back up again,
And God smiled.

Down through the seasons hot and cold,
We worshipped God together.
We'd thanked Him for our happy home,
Regardless of the weather,
And God smiled.

Artist of a Different Kind

I could not paint a mountain view,
Not even if I wanted to,
But I can have within my goals
To bring God's peace to troubled souls.

I could not sculpt a bust of clay
If I took lessons every day,
But I can give a word of cheer
That someone badly needs to hear.

I could not sing an aria,
Nor could I lead an orchestra,
But I can help a fallen friend
To find his way back home again.

I could not dance in a ballet,
Nor kick my heels in any way.
I can perform a thoughtful deed
Or help someone who is in need.

I could not play a grand piano,
A saxophone or tenor cello,
But I can always do my part
To show the world a caring heart.

Of all the arts there are to use,
The art of kindness will I choose.
I'll show His love in concrete ways
And pray my life to bring Him praise.

Come with Me

Follow Ma down the hillside
To her garden,
Where vines bend low,
Heavy with nature's bounty.
Help her gather
Red juicy tomatoes
And peppers,
Greener than the grasshoppers,
Hiding underneath them,
And pick, along with crisp green beans,
Tassled ears of corn.
Pile it all into
The pulled up skirt
Of her blue-flowered apron.
Trudge up the hill together,
And put all the vegetables
On the side of the sink.
Then go with Ma
Into the sloping side yard,
Where she'll wring
The neck of a plump chicken.
You can cover your eyes
If you want to
While the headless creature hops about.
She will let you help her
Pluck the chicken's feathers
And cut it into pieces
Before you flour it and fry it
In a huge iron skillet
Till it turns a golden brown.
She'll warn you to be careful
Not to let hot grease spatter
On your arms.
Then you can run away to play
While she kneads biscuits,
So light they might float away,

And she adds her magic touch to
The fresh picked vegetables.
After the family,
Gathered round the table,
Holds hands and says grace,
Ma will tell them
What a big help you were.
Then you can smile proudly.

Forever Sentry

I place a watch upon my heart
Lest seeds of bitterness should start
And grow until their flowers bloom,
Then all my peace and calm consume.
I'm not alone in this endeavor
Because the Holy Spirit ever
Within my secret heart does dwell,
And there He guards it very well.
It's He who does empower me
To be the person I should be.
He puts reminders in my way,
Encouragement for me to say
The words that He would have me speak,
Or even turn the other cheek
To one who's acted with unkindness,
And then present a kind of blindness
To the faults in every neighbor.
He instructs me how to labor
In good deeds of Christian duty
And reveal my inner beauty
Through decisions that I make
And the actions that I take.
I've a fount of love that's flowing
From the One who is all-knowing.
He loves me more than I deserve
And holds back nothing in reserve.
My heart I give Him in full measure,
Forever Sentry of my treasure.

Grandparents—Great, Great, and Beyond

I come from Scottish ancestry;
At least, that's what I'm told.
I've questions swirling in my mind
Of my forebears of old.

Did my ancestors long ago
Live royally in castles,
Or did they dwell in thatch-roofed homes
And did they serve as vassals?

Did they climb the high Munros
Or go fishing in the loch?
Did they catch a glimpse of Nessie
And then almost die of shock?

Did they ever toss a caber,
Dance a lively Highland fling,
Play a game of golf or rugby,
Or that squeaky bagpipe thing?

Did my progenitor wear kilts
To represent his clan,
And tuck a knife inside his sock,
As well-dressed Scottish man?

Did some drink potent potables
(Reports say many did),
Or hang with shady notables
Like well-known Captain Kidd?

Did young wee lads and lassies
(I am guessing this is sure),
Admire from a distance
Pretty thistles on the moor?

Whatever is my heritage
From Scotland's noble land,
Amazing is my pedigree
From lineage that is grand.

Ancestors that I've thought about
It would be fun to know.
Perhaps I'll meet some godly ones
In heaven when I go.

Growing-Old Charade

If I am only ten years old,
When did I get so tall,
And why do I walk now with care
For fear that I might fall?

It seems I might hear Mama call
"It's time to come to dinner,"
Or play a game of tag with friends,
And try to be the winner.

I'd like to run and skip and jump
And dance and shout with glee,
Or else to fly on roller skates
And climb the tall oak tree.

Though I'm not near as active
As I was a way back when,
I know the Lord is with me yet
As He has always been.

I wouldn't give up being Mom
Or Grandma, either one,
But I'd trade off my aching back
For little children's fun.

I might be a participant
In Growing-Old's parade,
But in my heart of hearts, I know
That's only a charade.

The truth I am compelled to tell
That cannot be denied:
No matter how I look or feel,
I'm still just ten inside.

Guess Who

Who shares my features' shape and size,
The color of my eyes?

Who has the same held memory
Of years that used to be?

Who recollects with me the ways
We spent our holidays?

Who knows the dumb things that I did
When I was just a kid?

Who was it that I fussed with, called them names,
When we played childhood games?

Who knows the love our parents had
When we were good or bad?

Who still remembers how Mom cooked
And how her kitchen looked?

Who sat with me when Daddy died
And held my hand and cried?

Who sends a loving birthday rhyme
On that day every time?

Who calls me on the phone to chat
With news of this and that?

Who shares a laugh for bygone years,
That's mingled with our tears?

Who feels the thread that binds my heart
When we are far apart?

You guessed, I'm sure, who it could be—
My siblings, dear to me.

I Go for a Dip

I dip just a toe
Into the ocean of inspiration.
Then dropping in my foot,
I draw a circle and
Watch the water whirl
Into ever-widening eddies
As I twirl my foot
Round and round.
I put both feet into the water
And wade,
Then kick a leg
And observe how the sun
Makes rich colored gems
Of the splashing droplets.
I step out farther
Until I am waist deep
In the sparkling sea.
I go farther yet,
Submerged up to my shoulders,
And hold onto earth
With my toes curled in the sand.
Now I swim out to the deep,
Not battling the current
Of the waves
That carry me in
And out again
to transport me to a distance
I had never thought to go.
I let myself rest in the power
And glide of the surging flow,
When I go under,
then come back up for air,
I laugh aloud
With the exhilaration
Of the ride.
Refreshed and energized,

Saturated with the passion
Of depths of inspiration,
I walk confidently to the shore.

Will You Still Hear Me Call Your Name?

Will you still hear me call your name
When I'm no longer here,
Imagining I'm by your side
Although I won't be near?

Will laughter we have shared for years
Still echo in your ears?
Will you remember when I wept
And how you dried my tears?

Will you recall our wedding day,
Our pledges to be true?
How voices shook in vows you made
And ones I made to you?

Will you hold dear the way we spoke
Of love for one another
And of the prayers we made to God
When we prayed with each other?

Will you forget the words I said,
Sometimes in thoughtlessness,
And think instead of memories
That bring you happiness?

Will you relive the countless hours
We spent in conversation,
The simple talks of day to day
And joys of celebration?

Then, if in God's own timing,
The worse will come to worst,
Your voice I'll hear for all my life,
If He should take you first.

In Apostle Paul's Footsteps

I walked on streets of marble where
Apostle Paul had been
And saw while in the land of Greece
The vistas that he'd seen.

The beautiful Aegean Sea,
With waves of greenish blue,
Was leaping high to catch the sun
Like playful children do.

Profusely grew the pomegranate,
The fig and olive trees,
Along with poppies, brightest red,
That swayed with every breeze.

Green valleys were abounding,
Where shepherds led their sheep
In shadows of gray mountains,
With inclines sharp and steep.

The temples and stone towers there
Were symbols of the story,
The monuments to bygone days
Of Grecian power and glory.

From harbors resting quietly
To cities that were walled,
I saw so many wondrous sights,
My senses were enthralled

I visited the ancient ruins,
Now under excavation,
And thought how Paul had been here once
To reach a Gentile nation.

I visualized his presence in
The ancient marketplace,
On stone steps and at synagogue,
Each step that I'd retrace.

So when I read the letters now
From Paul's inspired pen,
My heart recalls my journey, and
I'm back in Greece again.

Into the Lions' Den

Before I left the house, said he, my spouse who loves to tease,
"I know they will be shaking, so don't let them see your knees.
Your courage wrap around you, and be fearless from the start.
You're older than the lot of them and maybe twice as smart."

With such advice did I begin my challenging career.
An English teacher would I be if I could persevere.
Because I loved to read and write, this seemed the thing to do,
But now I wasn't quite so sure that I could carry through.

Outside the classroom door I stood, prepared to go inside
And wondered if it was too late for me to run and hide,
When suddenly before my eyes some paper airplanes flew.
The noise that echoed from the room filled me with fear anew.

I asked the Lord, "Are you quite sure that this should be my life?
You know just how upset I get with any kind of strife."
"Be still, my Daughter," came the words from Him to whom I'd prayed.
"When I am with you by your side, you need not be afraid."

So marched I in with steady step to be the one in charge,
Though I confess, the task I faced was looming mighty large.

My heart was beating double time; my hands were
    sweating, too.
It seemed to me I'd come to be the keeper of a zoo.

They were so busy talking that they hardly noticed me.
They had not come to school to learn, as near as I could
    see,
But I was made of sterner stuff, or so I had been told.
I knew I must be confident and positive and bold.

I cleared my throat and spoke to them as firmly as I
    could.
I hoped that they would listen and behave the way they
    should.
Then suddenly their talking stopped, and everyone was
    still.
I stood up straight and confident and started with a
    will.

Now many years have come and gone since that first
    teaching day,
And I can witness that the Lord's been with me all the
    way.
Thought of the fears I had that day, I never will forget,
The boldness that God gave me then is still part of me
    yet.

Kaleidoscope

Whirling, twirling . . . there I am.
I hold the kaleidoscope high as bright fragments
Congeal into pictures of shining memories,
Moments of music seen through a maze of years.

Whirling, twirling . . . there I am,
Held high in my preacher daddy's arms.
I lisp along with his loud clear voice,
"Jesus wants me for a sunbeam."

Whirling, twirling . . . there I am,
One in a group of children singing lustily,
"The B I B L E
Yes, that's the Book for me."

Whirling, twirling . . . there I am,
Standing beside the piano,
Totally enrapt with the music
That flows from my uncle's fingers.

Whirling, twirling . . . there I am,
Pretending to be a world-renowned musician.
I stand alone on the top church step
To present a special concert to imaginary crowds.

Whirling, twirling . . . there I am,
Listening to my mother as she sings.
She offers heartfelt praise to God
While she does her household chores.

Whirling, twirling . . . there I am,
Sitting at the old upright piano.
Mother always says that I practice best
When it's time to do the dishes.

Whirling, twirling . . . there I am,
A young lady singing the grand old hymns
At camp meetings and revivals
And Sunday-after-Sunday services.

Whirling, twirling . . . there I am,
Blending my voice in the college choir.
I revel in every note of the simplest song
To the awesome magnificence of "The Messiah."

Whirling, twirling . . . there I am.
Faster and faster the fragments blur,
Through love songs and lullabies
And sad songs sung with tear-filled eyes.

At last, the whirling, twirling stops,
And there I am
Amid a lifetime of Alleluias and Amens,
Blessed by amazing grace!

Lessons from the Grandchildren

Grandmothers know how God loves kids
Because we love them, too.
They are the treasures of our hearts,
No matter what they do.

Mine are the brightest of them all—
How could I not think so?
They've taught me lessons valuable
God wanted me to know.

Like Stephie, who, when she was three,
Spilled juice on my clean floor.
She said I'd not be mad at her
Because I loved her more.

And thus does God forgive my sin,
Whatever it might be.
His love is greater still by far;
His grace, completely free.

Sweet Allie sent a note to God,
She'd tied to red balloon.
Her message was that she loved Him.
She hoped He'd get it soon.

God wants me to communicate
As I seek Him in prayer,
To offer Him my praise and love
And give Him every care.

When Drew shopped with me for a cake,
He chose one from the rest
And said, "I'd get that one for God
'Cause it's the very best."

Now when I give my gifts to God,
I carefully must choose
The best of all things that I have
For Him to freely use.

Young Nolan waited on the porch
While we were hours away.
His mom had told him we'd be there
Much later in the day.

So do I wait with longing heart
And watch for Christ's return?
Do I work for Him all the while
And for His presence yearn?

These little ones showed me the way
God's kingdom is to be:
Life filled with hope and faithfulness,
With His love guiding me.

Now That Is a Great Adventure

And what is growing up,
But bumping and bruising
And falling down
And getting up again,
Yet knowing every day
That the God
Of all the universe
Is watching over you?
Now that is a great adventure!

And what is getting married,
But bumping and bruising
And falling down
And getting up again together,
Yet knowing every day
That the God
Of all the universe
Is watching over you both?
Now that is a great adventure!

And what is having children,
But watching them bump and bruise
And fall down
And get up again,
Yet, knowing every day
That the God
Of all the Universe
Is watching over them?
Now that is a great adventure!

And what is growing old,
But bumping and bruising
And falling down
And *sometimes* getting up again,
Still knowing every day
That the God

Of all the universe
Is watching over you?
Now that is a great adventure!

Picture of a Queen

She enters her kingdom
Of savory scents,
Where she rules
As sole monarch.
She first invites,
Through her CD's,
Singers and musicians
To inspire
And entertain her.
She sings along
With grand old hymns
While she prepares
Her family's favorites,
With a heaping help
Of chocolate.
As she chops and minces,
Stirs and mixes,
Fries and bakes,
She prays—
First offering thanks
For every blessing,
Then petitioning
God to help,
Guide, and protect
Each one of
Her dearly loved ones,
Dwelling longest
On the one
With greatest need.
She delights in seeing
Her family,
All together around her table,
Teasing, laughing,
Sharing anecdotes.
Then after meals,
While cleaning up,

She plays her
Favorite oldies
And sometimes
Does a little dance
When no one's
There to watch.
When husband steals
Into her realm
With kisses and a hug,
She's glad this is the life
That God prepared
For her.
She's happy to be
The queen of her domain.

Shivering and Shuddering

I shivered in my boots to hear
The heartbeat 'neath the floor
And listened to the raven when
He quoted "Nevermore."

I held my breath in horror
At poor Fortunato's end—
To be bricked up behind a wall
By vengeful, jealous friend.

I wept some tears for Annabel
In crypt there by the sea
And wondered at the sadness of
Love destined not to be.

I shuddered with disgust at one
With such a wretched life,
He'd grimly hang his fat black cat
And axe his loving wife.

I quaked with fear at seeing in
The mad barbaric revel,
Unmasking of the Red Death as
A dark decaying devil.

All this I did while reading from
That famous author, Poe,
Whose morbid fancies often led
To places I'd not go.

Indeed, a gifted writer, he,
With creativity.
Did write of sin and sadness with
Supreme ability.

If I had Poe's great talent,
I would write so folks could read
How God's grace has sufficiency
To meet each person's need.

Snapshots from a Teacher's Album

There it is . . .
In the morning in black magic marker,
"Maurice loves Kendra 4-ever"
Scrawled on the shiny desk.
Too bad their forever love
Doesn't last till late afternoon.

There he is . . .
Hopping on his single leg
To the pencil sharpener
To dance a happy impromptu jig.
Cancer has claimed his leg,
But not his indomitable spirit.

There she is . . .
Tardy to class again,
Exploding into the room
With a burst of giggles,
Flamboyant, fun-loving—
My practice for patience.

There they are . . .
Amid plates of pizza and French fries,
Boisterous voices bouncing
Against cafeteria walls,
Tomorrow's flowers
Budding in the garden of today.

There I am among them . . .
They color my life with indelible crayons,
And for all the lessons I teach
Of prose and poetry,
I pray they learn from me
The art of kindness.

She Said

She said:
You can't go there.
You can't wear that.
You can't do that.
You can't say that,

And I was sad.

Then after the passage
Of many years
Of making my own choices,

She said:
I can't sing anymore.
I can't drive a car anymore.
I can't cook anymore.
I can't live in my house anymore,

And I was very, very sad.

What Is It?

Is it hid within my elbow?
Could it be beneath my knee?
Might it even rest upon my face
For everyone to see?

It hears what my ears hear.
It sees what my eyes see.
It beats within my heart
And breathes along with me.

It is in my joys and sorrows,
In my smiles and in my tears.
It is in my hopes and dreams,
In my life through all my years.

It is in the truth I speak,
In the character I show,
Though it's hidden deep inside me,
It goes every place I go.

It is filled with my desire
When I seek my Lord above,
As I ask Him for His favor
And I give to Him my love.

For it rests in my salvation,
In redemption that will bring,
And it prompts my life to service,
Always, only for my King.

It offers praise each day to Him
Who made my heart sin-free.
It looks toward my promised life
With Him eternally.

It's really not a mystery—
It's soul and spirit that makes "me."
God breathed it there inside my heart
As part of mankind's legacy.

Family

www.ingramcontent.com/pod-product-compliance
Lightning Source LLC
Chambersburg PA
CBHW031355040426
42444CB00005B/304